PRAISE FOR *Not One Thing*

What a delight to travel with Carolyn Locke as she follows Basho's "Narrow Road to the Interior" with her open heart, notebook and camera, and hat with lavender in the hatband. She encounters a landscape rich with thousands of years of ghosts, mists, forests, fields, rain, and "ancient stories forever rising." These stories rise into her heart, "finding the unchanging within the changing," "following paths the gods passed over."

Loosened from this life, and wandering, "we enter the flow of the universe"—and the universe changes, and Carolyn's understanding of the universe changes, as she follows Basho into the Interior.

Using Basho as a guide, a mapmaker, a mentor, Carolyn follows his poems "as a diary of the heart"—writing her own poems, letting us read her heart, sharing her own journey. She tells us, "We are in search of history, but I am focussed on the old man harvesting potatoes and the woman cutting cabbage, on birdsong in the fields and the magenta phlox that makes me long for home."

Basho says, "Every day is a journey and the journey is home."

Carolyn says,

> "Even walking on
> this narrow road, I long for
> this narrow road."

Carolyn takes us on a journey to the Interior, to the heart, a journey home.

—GARY LAWLESS, author of *Caribouddhism*, *In Ruins*, *Nanao or Never*, and *Two Owls*

Not One Thing

*Following Matsuo Basho's
Narrow Road to the Interior*

Carolyn Locke

Permissions to reprint portions of other publications

Awesome Nightfall: The Life, Times, and Poetry of Saigyo by William Lafleur. © 2003 Wisdom Publications, www.wisdompubs.org. Reproduced by permission of Wisdom Publications.

Excerpt from "Little Gidding" from *Four Quartets* by T.S. Eliot. © 1942 by Houghton Mifflin Harcourt Publishing Company; © renewed by T. S. Eliot. Reprinted by permission of Houghton Mifflin Harcourt Publishing Company. All rights reserved.

From *Narrow Road to the Interior by Matsuo Basho*, translated by Sam Hamill. © 1991 by Sam Hamill. Reprinted by arrangement with Shambhala Publications Inc., Boston, MA. www.shambhala.com.

How To Live on the Planet Earth by Nanao Sakaki. © 2013 Blackberry Books. Reprinted by permission of Blackberry Books.

The Narrow Road to the Deep North and Other Travel Sketches by Matsuo Basho translated with an introduction by Nobuyuki Yuasa (Penguin Classics, 1966). © 1966 Nobuyuki Yuasa. Reproduced by permission of Penguin Books Ltd.

Turning Toward the Morning © 1975, Gordon Bok, BMI.

ISBN 978-1-938883-25-5

Book designed and produced by
Maine Authors Publishing
Rockland, Maine
www.maineauthorspublishing.com

For Gerry, whose generosity and wisdom
in letting me go has always brought me home again

—with love and appreciation

Acknowledgments

This book reflects a personal journey, but I had many companions along the way to whom I owe a great deal.

I offer heartfelt thanks to Laurel Rasplica Rodd for the journey that gave birth to this book and for her enthusiastic support of its publication; to my Fulbright Hays traveling companions for their unfailing good humor and inspiration; and to the many Japanese people, too numerous to name, who opened their hearts and shared their culture with us along the way.

I would also like to recognize several writing companions who read and commented on this manuscript at various stages and whose insights and support were invaluable in the process of revision: Ellen Goldsmith, Chrystal Wing, Lucinda Garthwaite, Jim Reed, Judy Williams, and Helen Tirone. A special thanks goes to Jim Clark, who not only critiqued the manuscript but also designed the map insert. I am also grateful to the members of the Goddard College Clockhouse Writers Conference who listened to me read and offered encouragement.

As always, I offer love and thanks to special friends and family: Linda Lord, who read the manuscript with enthusiasm and gave me the courage to keep going; friends Sheila Gilluly, Tanya Hubbard, and Carol Dennington, and my sisters, Ann Lamper and Sylvia Millett, who have always been there for me; and especially my family—Gerry, Jeff, and Alison—who have always supported my travel and writing adventures.

Thanks also to Jane Karker and the team at Maine Authors Publishing, especially David Allen for his hard work on the design of the book, Genie Dailey for her editing work, and Cheryl McKeary for helping with logistics.

Finally, I owe much to writers who have gone before me—especially Basho, Issa, Saigyo, Nanao Sakaki, T. S. Eliot, Mary Oliver, and Mark Strand—who became my spiritual companions on this journey.

INTRODUCTION

I remember the moment clearly—a December morning in 2008 when I was monitoring a high school study hall. Not anxious to begin reading the stack of papers I'd carried with me, I began idly thumbing through a newsletter on Asian studies from the Five College Center in Northampton, Massachusetts. There it was: the trip I'd been dreaming about since I had left Japan in July of 2002. As a participant in a three-week Fulbright Memorial Fund program that summer, I had been given the experience of a lifetime—learning about Japanese culture and education, visiting schools and colleges, and spending a weekend with a Japanese family on Amamioshima. On my final night in Tokyo, I read Dorothy Britton's translation of Matsuo Basho's *A Haiku Journey: Narrow Road to a Far Province*. This journal of his travels through northern Honshu in 1689, which combined prose and poetry, affected me so deeply that I opened my own journal and wrote: "If I ever return to Japan, the one thing I'd like to do is follow Basho's travels."

Settling back into my home in Maine, I set my dream aside and began sharing my Japanese experiences with family, friends, students, fellow teachers, and the community. Over the next six years, my respect and love for Japanese culture deepened. At the same time, I taught and pursued opportunities to expand my learning to other Asian cultures by taking courses, attending workshops, and traveling twice to China with an organization called Primary Source. Still, I yearned to return to Japan.

Now, six years later, Laurel Rasplica Rodd, the director of the Center for Asian Studies at the University of Colorado, was calling for applications for a Fulbright-Hays Group Projects Abroad Seminar to Japan. Sixteen teachers from kindergarten through post-secondary levels would be selected for this month-long "Journey to the Interior," during which they would study Basho's famous journal of the same name, write their own journals and haiku, and travel through northern Honshu, following in the footsteps of one of Japan's greatest poets. Could this be real? Quickly, I re-read the description and qualifications for applicants, e-mailed Laurel to reassure myself that I did indeed meet the qualifications, and sat stunned when her reply was positive. Could my impossible dream actually happen?

When I received the news that I had been accepted

for the project, I couldn't believe it. This was meant to be a trip for educators to learn about Basho and Japanese culture and to develop units of study for their classrooms. For me, however, it was already so much more. In some strange way, during my years of teaching and study, I had begun to feel as if a part of me was Japanese. When I read a wonderful haiku or looked at a painting or piece of pottery, I felt a gentle quietness settling in, as if I had arrived home. I knew this journey would feed my soul and allow me to use my skills as a poet to write from the heart. It seemed to me that I had been preparing for this all of my life. My travels, my education, my teaching, all the years of writing poems, and my MFA in Creative Writing had brought me to this place. I was ready.

I soon received a bibliography and packet of readings from Laurel, and for the next three months immersed myself in learning more about Basho and the Edo period during which he lived. At that time, Japan was largely isolated from the outside world, and partially because of that, its unique culture and the traditional arts flourished. Basho's early work suggests that he was a product of a long-established tradition of poets, diarists, and travel writers. However, as he aged and experienced sadness and loss, he turned to Zen Buddhism and began to retreat, shedding the trappings of society for a simpler life and writing poems of greater depth. When he set off for the north with his companion Sora in 1689, he assumed the clothing of a humble monk. Traveling on foot, he became closer to nature and the lives of ordinary people, visited historic and religious sites, explored the richness of Japanese culture, and sought to understand the passage of time. Although his wanderings were grounded in time and place, he was in search of the eternal in the ephemeral world. The physical hardships of his journey were many. In fact, he hadn't expected to survive the trip, suggesting that this pilgrimage must have been essential to his very being. Otherwise, why take such risk?

The more I learned about Basho and his world, the more deeply I was able to read his journal and make connections with my own life experience: the way poetry is woven into my life, defining my very existence; my insatiable need to travel; my desire for lonely solitude; the way I love to wander through a day, seeking a rhythm that somehow connects me with something larger than myself. I thought about the varied translations of the Japanese title *Oku No Hosomichi*: *Narrow Road to the Interior*; *A Haiku Journey: Narrow Road to a Far Province*; *The Narrow Road Through the Provinces*. Each one suggested much more than a physical journey, reminding me of a quote from T. S. Eliot's "Four Quartets" that I first read in 1969 and have carried with me ever since:

> We shall not cease from exploration
> And the end of all our exploring
> Will be to return where we started
> And know the place for the first time. (197)

I was excited to begin my own humble wanderings through Japan. How would Basho's experience of the world be woven into my own? What other threads would be added? Already, my perceptions of the universe and my place in it were beginning to shift like multicolored glass pieces in a kaleidoscope.

* * *

Our group's journey began in Los Angeles on June 28, 2009, where we assembled to develop a common pool of knowledge and learn about each other. Two days later, we departed for Narita, Japan. Upon our arrival, we traveled to Urawa, the base for our day trips into Tokyo to visit Basho-related sites and to learn more about the Edo period. Finally, on July 5, our northward journey began. Like Basho, we would

visit many famous religious and historic sites, hike through some of the countryside, and meet many people along the way. Each encounter would help us in our search to better understand Japanese culture and values, both past and present.

Our first stop was Nikko, site of the Toshogu, a mortuary shrine built for Tokugawa Ieyasu, first leader of the Tokugawa Shogunate that ruled Japan from 1600 until 1867. From there we moved on to Kurobane, Sendai, Shiogama, Matsushima, and Hiraizumi, finally crossing the Shitomae Barrier on July 14. During Basho's lifetime this was a literal and symbolic passage into the wilderness frontier and the entrance into the Dewa Province, home of the sacred mountains of the Yamabushi, whose religious practice, called Shugendo, is based on a fusion of esoteric Buddhism and Shinto beliefs. Next, we journeyed south and west to Yamagata and Yamadera, where we climbed the 1,015 steps of a Tendai Buddhist mountain temple and explored the sacred mountains of Haguro, Gassan, and Yudono-san. After a boat trip down the Mogami River, we reached the west coast, staying briefly in Sakata and then traveling south along the Japan Sea to Kanazawa. Heading south through the island to the Shima Peninsula on the Pacific coast, we reached our final stop before returning to Urawa: Ise, home of the most sacred Shinto shrines in Japan.

During this 1500-mile journey, I wrote feverishly, sometimes taking notes as we walked or scribbling during train rides. I stayed up at night to review the photographs I'd taken during the day and to record my thoughts and feelings. I composed haiku nearly every day, starting with one journal, then adding a smaller notebook that fit in my camera case so I could write easily whenever something caught my attention, and finally expanding to a large notebook for the revision of haiku. By the time I returned home, I had six different vessels filled with words, hundreds of photographs on my camera's memory card, and a mind and heart full of things Japanese.

Next came the exhilarating task of putting together my own journal. What you will find here is a work of love that explores and honors one woman's encounter with one of the world's most incredible cultures as well as her journey into her own interior world. Written in the form of haibun—a combination of prose, haiku, and images—it does not pretend to be an academic study, nor does it offer a complete explanation of all terms, concepts, and historical references. Instead, it strives to be brief and open-ended, allowing for leaps of the imagination and individual interpretation. Perhaps it will send you on your own journey into Japanese culture, where you will discover yourself anew.

The moon and the sun are eternal travelers. Even the years wander on. A lifetime adrift in a boat or in old age leading a tired horse into the years, every day is a journey and the journey itself is home.

(Matsuo Basho as translated in Hamill, 3)

8. Kisakata

17. Sakata
16. Mogami River

8. Hiraizumi

13. Mount Haguro

9. Akakura Onsen

14. Gassan
15. Yudono-san

10. Obanazawa
7. Matsushima

12. Yamadera
6. Shiogama

11. Yamagata
5. Sendai

SEA OF JAPAN

3. Nikko   4. Kurobane

19. Kanazawa

HONSHU
2. Urawa
1. Tokyo

20. Ise

Our Journey
Following
Okunohosomichi
in 2009

How to mark the beginning of this journey? Where to break into the flow of time and say, "Yes. This is where it all began"?

Perhaps it was on July 4, 2002 at the Century Hyatt Hotel in Tokyo, when I first read Basho's journal and imagined following his journey. Or maybe it began as far back as the moment Basho set foot on the road north in 1689. Could it even reach back to the twelfth century journeys of the poet Saigyo, one of Basho's literary heroes, or before that to...? How startling to realize that my footsteps are about to merge with many others on this journey that I will carry with me into the future. Where will my footsteps take me? How will this journey change my view of the world? How will it change me?

JUNE 25, 2009

This morning, three days before my travels begin, I am reading Earl Miner's translation of Basho's *The Narrow Road Through the Provinces*:

> ...my heart was burdened by the thought of the many miles stretching ahead, and my tears fell over

such parting on the illusory path of this world. (158) I knew that the sufferings of travel are said to bring a fall of frost to one's head...still, there were places I had heard of but had not seen. (158)

These thoughts echo through my mind during my final preparations for the trip.

Blue sandal straps
bind my feet—elusive birds
longing for mountain clouds.

JUNE 28, 2009

Today I set off from Maine for Los Angeles, already missing home.

Heavy summer rains—
sweet scent of heliotrope
brushing bare skin.

Days without sun, nights
without moon, woodpecker still
hammers the weathered pole.

And imagining the road ahead:

Silver ropes twist
in the wind, sail masts shiver—
Matsushima dreams.

JUNE 29, 2009

A day of orientation and waiting. The group reviews the itinerary, course content, and expectations; shares stories of past travels and the most surprising things we've ever done; learns a little Japanese language; and discusses curriculum plans. In spite of the wonderful camaraderie and conversation, the day fades quickly during an evening walk on Olivera Street.

Three bells, two crosses
against an orange sky—footsteps
under the half moon.

This journey will take me through a full cycle of the moon, the same moon Saigyo wrote about over eight hundred years ago.

We would together
make our journey, I on land
and it in the sky.
If the moon comes out to stay,
empathy both ways.

(as translated in LaFleur, 90)

JUNE 30—JULY 1, 2009

Today (and tomorrow, so it seems), we travel to Tokyo.

Lost in transit—this
silver capsule streaking
across endless sky.

I enter the world of Alex Kerr's *Lost Japan* and place quotes on the empty pages of my journal to encounter during my wanderings.

> *jo, ha, kyu, zanshin*…amounting to slow, faster, fast, stop…the closing *zanshin* means "leaving behind the heart"…[this rhythm] is the fundamental rhythm of nature—it defines the destinies of men, the course of eras, even the growth of galaxies, and the very ebb and flow of the universe. (112)
> One eventually has no choice but to…surrender to the serenity of the empty room. (43)

Drifting off to sleep, I hear my heart beating quietly in that empty room.

Arrival in Tokyo is a flurry of activity: reassemble our bleary-eyed group; go through customs; get train passes and Japanese yen; hop a train to Urawa; walk through a maze of dark and unfamiliar streets to the Japan Foundation, our home base while we are in Japan. A restless night's sleep follows, my body still experiencing the forward momentum of the plane.

JULY 2, 2009

A whirlwind review of Japanese history, religion, language, and customs. Preliterate Japan c. 4000 B.C. to 300 A.D. spanned the Jomon, Yayoi, and Tomb periods. Around 552, the introduction of Buddhism. From 710 to 814, the Nara period followed by the Heian, the Kamakura, the Kemmu Restoration. And we've only reached 1336, some three hundred years before Basho's Tokugawa, Japan, which itself lasted 250 years. And on and on the history goes, intermingled with complicated religious movements—Shinto, Daoism, Confucianism, Buddhism in its many manifestations (Shingon, Tendai, Pure Land, Nichiren, Zen, Rinzai Zen, Dogen). And remember, please, to begin speaking Japanese at mealtimes and in between: *itadakimasu* (humble acceptance <u>before</u> eating); *gochisosamadeshita* (humble praise for the meal <u>after</u> eating); *osewa ni narimasu* (a thank-you for any time you feel you are being well taken care of); *arigato* (a simple thank-you); *domo arigato* (thank you very much); *domo arigato gozaimasu* (thank you very very much); *ohayo gozaimasu* (greeting for the morning); *konnichiwa* (greeting for the afternoon); *konbanwa* (greeting for the evening); *sayonara* (a formal good-bye); *ja mata* (an informal good-bye). And don't forget to pass your business card with two hands (with your name facing the person), remember always to wrap gifts, and never, ever forget to bow. I am terrified I will not remember one thing. Where is the serenity of that empty room?

JULY 3, 2009

We visit the Edo Tokyo Museum, where Japan's history unfolds in vivid displays. At the entrance, miniature street scenes filled with jugglers, men dancing in bright yellow masks, parades, children chasing chickens and dogs, merchants selling their goods, large crowds mingling. I imagine walking in the carnival atmosphere of these streets beside Basho and Sora as they ready themselves for their journey.

From room to room, the images build. Devastating floods, earthquakes, and fires. Ordinary people—eating, cooking, sleeping, working the fields, making crafts, caring for the sick, creating music. Pilgrims and monks traveling winding paths to sacred shrines. Fearsome facial masks and the protective armor of the samurai. Powerful leaders sending men to war. The stunning transformation of parts of Tokyo into a model Western city during the Meiji Restoration. Tokyo in ruins after the fire bombings of World War II. Hiroshima. Nagasaki. Japan's rise to a modern industrial power. Skyscrapers. Telecommunications. Layers and layers. Thousands of years of history.

What is it that drives mankind? What pushes us to glorious creation or to mass destruction?

> *jo, ha, kyu,*
> *zanshin—endlessly seeking*
> *rhythm at the core.*

After lunch, we take a walking tour of the Fukagawa area where Basho lived before he set off for the Deep North. We visit Fukagawa Fudo Temple, where I buy a temple book and have it signed in calligraphy by one of the monks. This will be my most precious souvenir: for each religious site, a unique flow of brushstrokes resting on the serene emptiness of the page.

Next we walk through the grounds of Tomioka Hachiman Shrine with its stone tablets engraved with the names of sumo wrestlers in long columns and its monuments into which the huge hand- and footprints of generations of famous sumo wrestlers have been pressed. So many footsteps to follow here.

Today we stroll along the Sumida River where Basho's poems are carved in stone.

> The full moon—
> circumambulating the pond
> all night long.

We stop at the studio of Oishi Sensei, a renowned calligrapher, who has offered to give a lesson in his art. Although I appreciate his generous gift, the quick lesson is too quick for my slow nature. When he says it is time, I am not ready to defile a perfectly white fan with my unpracticed strokes. Later, I read two quotes from Kerr, strategically placed in my journal: "Calligraphy is a portrait of the heart …"(126) and "Wine is the perfect companion to calligraphy." (129) Perhaps the absence of wine was the problem. Or maybe I wasn't ready for the revelation of the heart…

In the afternoon we are met by Mr. Fumio Ichihara, Director of the Okunohosomichi Network. He has arranged for a boat ride down the Sumida River (complete with tea ceremony) to Senju, where Basho officially began his journey. When we disembark, just as Basho's friends

did for him centuries ago, members of the Network wave to us until we are out of sight. We have just met, but still I feel as if I'm leaving a part of my heart with them.

Buddhism teaches that "… all things are fully dependent even at the point of origin …" (Hamill, xi) and that "The 'self' is empty of independent existence."(Hamill, xi) I'm just beginning to understand.

I observe people walking and bicycling down this road and think about threads tying them to the past and spinning out into the future. "Those who remain behind watch the shadow of a traveler's back disappear." (Basho as translated by Hamill, 4) What am I leaving behind? Who is watching?

Cycles within cycles. They say seven is a lucky number. Seven years ago today, my first trip to Japan was at an end, and I was on a plane, dreaming about a return to follow Okunohosomichi. Simultaneously, Laurel Rasplica Rodd was on her first Okunohosomichi trip with students from the University of Colorado. What forces have been at play over those seven years to bring us together on this train headed for Nikko?

And this is the year of the ox, the fifth cycle of twelve years since I was born in 1949. It feels like an auspicious beginning.

Sora, Basho's companion on his journey, "changed his clothes" in Nikko. Sam Hamill says that Basho "patched his old cotton trousers and repaired his straw hat" (ix), and began a long journey "into the geography of the soul." (xxxi) I humbly hope for the same.

We arrive in heavy rain, receiving summer greetings:

> *Butterfly wanders*
> *among white hydrangeas—*
> *mountain waters calling.*

Everywhere we encounter bamboo branches hung with brightly colored strips of paper on which people have written their wishes for Tanabata. This is the one night on which, according to legend, Cowherd Star (Altair) and Weaver Star (Vega), lovers separated by the Milky Way, are allowed to meet.

I write my secret wish on a a strip of soft orchid paper and hang it from an empty branch.

We spend the afternoon wandering the Toshogu, a mortuary shrine built for Tokugawa Ieyasu, founder of the Tokugawa Shogunate, which ruled Japan for more than 250 years beginning in 1600. The smell of incense permeates the heavy air, and moss covers the stone lanterns, called toro. White prayer papers hang like laundry between feathered branches on the path leading toward the temple. A drenching downpour sends us for cover in a shelter filled with chattering women and giggling children. In spite of my desire for a solitary experience, the press of bodies is pleasant. When the rain finally lets up, we continue on, stopping inside the temple to witness a Buddhist ritual as mysterious and uplifting as the Latin Catholic masses of my childhood. We wander through several other buildings, finding a souvenir shop, where I purchase a silver necklace engraved with the sign of the ox. Good omens abound.

Late in the afternoon, we walk past our lodgings at the Turtle Inn and saunter along the river, where we are surprised by a long row of stone Jizo wearing hand-knit red caps and red cotton bibs. Believed to safeguard those in transit from one world to another, Jizo are especially important to women who have lost children. They protect the dead, and here they provide the only brightness in the dark, rain-soaked woods.

Reluctantly, I leave them behind and follow worn stone steps curving up and into the hillside to a cemetery filled with markers and statues of deceased Shingon

priests. Moss covering the stones and ferns growing out of their heads are a poignant reminder of the passage of time. Headed back to the inn, I hear the cuckoo call from the woods and whisper to myself Basho's famous haiku about Kyoto. In his rhythms, I discover my own.

Even walking on
this narrow road, I long for
this narrow road.

Completely relaxed by my first Japanese hot bath, I fall asleep to the sounds of the river rushing toward the sea and follow in my dreams.

The first morning birds, joining voices one by one, call me back.

Outside the window
a red roof, slick with misty
mountain tears.

Before breakfast, I return alone to the Jizo along the river. Who dressed them and why? Where are those women now?

Jizo caps—red flames
lit by lonely hands along
the flowing river.

I think of the baby I lost over thirty years ago.

Somewhere in mountain
mists, a quiet heart follows
my fading footsteps.

When I return to the inn, I am glad to have the company of the group. We spend the morning climbing up to Urami-no-taki, where Basho wrote his now famous poem about standing inside the waterfall.

> Stopped awhile
> inside a waterfall—
> summer retreat begins.
>
> (as translated in Hamill, 6)

Two intrepid members of our group brave the slippery wet slope to stand where Basho once did, cleansing themselves in the water's spray. I watch, envious of their lighthearted bravery, yet unable to ignore the heavy weight of water crashing below.

> *Rushing falls tumble*
> *over steep cliffs, pooling deep*
> *in these trembling bones.*

I opt out of an afternoon trip back to Toshogu and instead wander alone along the Daiya River and through Nikko National Park.

> *Black and white—unnameable*
> *bird on a rain-worn stone:*
> *softness!*

Old Shinto shrines are tucked in among cryptomeria trees whose trunks are so large that it would take several people joining hands to reach around their circumference.

> *These trunks reaching*
> *skyward—how far their*
> *roots must spread beneath us.*

> *White prayers quiver*
> *above trickling waters—fingers*
> *washing the worn cup.*

Again I feel called by the Jizo and return to them before dark. I stare into their stone faces for a long time. What do they see, these guardians of travelers on The Way? What is the essence of life that transforms itself before them again and again, like river waters returning to the sea?

Tanabata stars
hidden behind Nikko's clouds—
cicadas whirring.

Tanabata Festival Day. On this night, will the Cowherd and the Weaver meet in the sky? Will all wishes come true? During our final moments in Nikko, something is shifting.

Morning explodes
in golden dragonflies—sunlight
on deep green leaves.

I dream of watching tonight's full moon rise, and as we travel to Kurobane, I resolve to follow the advice on a Zen gate: "I'll not say anything foolish, just the joy of living gratefully."

Members of the Global Culture Nasu meet us at the train station and usher us into a lovely hotel where the way of tea is presented, this time in great detail and with much ceremony. Clearly, our experience on the river in Tokyo had only hinted at the real thing.

A handout shows us the eight steps to be followed before drinking the tea, offers a description of the proper way to drink from the cup, and explains three steps to follow after drinking. In addition, we are given a list of twelve Japanese terms for the tea service set and several words related to the theme of today's tea, which is waterfalls, in honor of our recent trip to Urami-no-Taki. In *Lost Japan,* Alex Kerr says, "A Kanji is surrounded by a cloud of meaning, like the colors radiating from the halo of a Buddha." (123) The same could be said for the way of tea. Mystery and layers of meaning abound everywhere we turn.

writers (such as Yosano Akiko, Masaoka Shiki, Tanizaki Junichiro, and Akutagawa) who, like Basho, wrote poems and left them for the innkeepers. The owner lifts precious poetry manuscripts painted on silk from wooden boxes and allows us to examine and photograph them.

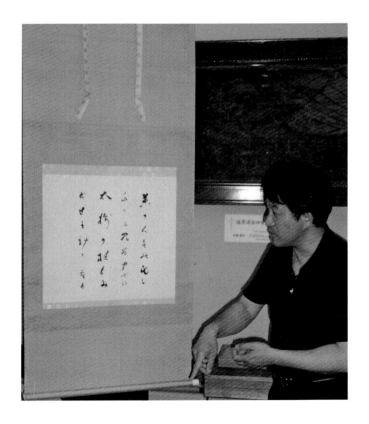

Next, we are bused into the mountains, where we visit the Shiobara Literature Center and meet with the owner of the Masuya Inn. Run by the same family for generations, this inn has sheltered many twentieth-century poets and

Although I can't read the words, I know they were written by men and women who followed Basho at least in part. They came here to be inspired by the beauty of the mountains and hot springs, and to escape the strict morality of Tokyo, finding truth in a more earthy existence.

We are told that many inns in the area hold such treasures. More layers, more mysteries.…

Our hosts have arranged for a hot springs foot bath and massage where smooth stones soothe our weary feet. Like Basho, we find the residents of Kurobane hospitable and remarkably concerned with our every comfort.

One of my companions and I are picked up by Mr. Watanabe and his son Atsume. Both are insurance agents and drummers. Watanabe-san, Atsume confides, is an "old-school drummer," while he is more contemporary. They bring us to the home of Mr. Watanabe's sister, where there is no time for introductions. Our meal is waiting. A videotape is set to run on the television, and our homestay begins in delightful chaos.

Flurry of greeting hands—
sit for a feast! Urami
waters joining us.

We watch images of Basho's visit to Nikko and Urami Falls unfold on the screen while Mr. Watanabe's sister, his niece, and a friend jabber in delight. We do our best to hold up our end of the conversation. Asked if he writes haiku, Atsume responds, "No, but I like to hike!" and throws his head back in laughter. And so the evening goes. Atsume sings his praises for Kurt Vonnegut, "favorite American author," and whips out a picture of him.

The women begin pulling kimono out of ceiling-high chests—a lovely three-season pink, a black-and-white winter with Tokugawa scenes woven into it, and a pink-and-cream striped for casual wear. They tie on obis, don kimono socks and platform zori, and parade around the room. Watanabe-san sits at the table engrossed in text-

messaging while Atsume hovers around the women, giggling and offering compliments and halting translations as needed.

Without warning, Watanabe-san stands up and indicates that he and Atsume will be leaving. Only the women and Mokichi, the cat, remain to host us for the night. We quickly set out our futons on the tatami mat and turn out the lights, high chests of kimono looming over us in the dark.

JULY 8, 2009

Mokichi wakes us early, and a morning as baffling as the previous evening ensues.

Watanabe-san and Atsume join us for a traditional Japanese breakfast of many dishes: crisp tempura, pickles, rice, fresh fish, and miso soup. Then they whisk us away to their office, where we are served a concoction of shaved ice, strawberry syrup, and cream that mysteriously appears after a racket of grinding has emanated from a tiny back room. Abruptly, Watanabe-san flips on some rock music, sits down to his butter-yellow drum set, and begins to play.

As a parting gift, Atsume gives us each a CD of music selections entitled *Music for My American People*. Then WHOOSH!! We are back in the car and on our way to meet up with our companions, some of whom, unlike us, have had the luxury of gazing at the full moon the night before. Truly, no haiku could do this homestay justice.

Back on the bus with volunteers from the Global Culture Nasu, we head for an experience of an entirely different sort, this time to Unganji, the Zen temple that Basho visited and where he found the remains of his teacher Priest Buccho's hermitage. Once again, I read the words he wrote there:

> Even the woodpeckers
> Have left it untouched,
> This tiny cottage
> In a summer grove.
>
> (as translated in Yuasa, 104)

I remember the woodpecker in my own poem written before leaving on this journey and marvel at the energies and powers of the universe which surely connect us all.

As I stroll the temple area, I'm calmed by the sensation of circular motion: a swirl of mountain breezes echoed in curving rooftops; swaying pine branches; crow call spiraling overhead; my slow steps over worn stones strewn with moist brown leaves.

The presence of my companions has faded into the distant mountains. I fall into a deep silence as I stare at a wooden tablet hanging from the temple. For hundreds of years, it has been the sole means of communication among the monks living here.

Now, only one monk inhabits the temple.

Last monk in the curve
of wind—lonely trout swimming
the Nakagawa.

I would prefer to remain here for the rest of the day, but we are called back to the bus and head for the Kurobane castle ruins and "Basho-related sites," such as Basho-no-michi poetry monuments, the reconstructed home of Basho's disciple Joboji, and a Basho museum, where we are once again shown the way of tea. The hills around these sites are filled with hydrangeas blooming in shades of blue, pink, and purple, and the sound of a stringed instrument travels down the path.

Kurobane hills:
among blue hydrangeas
stone tablets whisper—
shamisen strings pulling north
the full Okinawa moon.

Half moon in the grain—
scent of white camellias*
beneath the mallet.

*Note: the Japanese word for *camellia* is translated as "no mouth."

25

Such a full day already, it is hard to believe that we still have a train ride north to Sendai, a thoroughly modern city with a very long history.

Bees buzzing along
steel rails, what pollen draws them
to this old flower?

July 9, 2009

I sit quietly by an open door in the common room of the Dochuan Youth Hostel.

Rain patters on leaves
coolness caressing my feet—
another journey.

I read about Basho's arrival in Sendai on May the fourth, the day on which people throw iris leaves on their roofs. They pray for good health and believe the smell of iris repels snakes. Here, too, Basho was given a pair of sandals corded with iris-blue thongs.

I look at my own feet bound in blue-strapped sandals and smile, remembering an encounter with a snake on the river path in Nikko.

Old snake resting
on the path—did he catch the scent
of my blue sandals?

Just as the artist Kaemon escorted Basho to various places of interest around Sendai, Mr. Yoshikawa, aged 74 and appropriately dressed in purple jacket and lavender pants, guides us in pouring rain around the town and through gorgeous gardens of purple iris.

Blue umbrellas bob
along the road—shy flowers
bowing to the iris.

Through the increasingly heavy rain, I watch a white crane wading in the Tamagawa.

I remember Basho's poem about a crane standing in the spring rain. How patiently this crane sits while we make our way along the shore.

Stillness—a white crane
in the Tamagawa, rain
falling on folded wings.

Sight after sight moves me. I fervently wish for several arms, not to use in prayer, but to juggle umbrella, camera, notebook, and pen in a futile attempt to capture each moment before it passes.

Pine dripping over
moss-covered stone—iris gone
to seed by the well.

Widow's tears closing
beneath hidden stars—is my love
gazing at the sky?

We make our way to the excavated ruins of Tagajo Castle. Erected in 762, it lasted only twenty years as a frontier fortress against "the barbarians" during the Nara period. Because of its evocation of history a thousand years before his time, the site moved Basho to tears. I put my feet to the task of climbing the stairs to Seicho, the place of official ceremonies at Tagajo. Thinking of Issa's famous poem about the snail climbing Mount Fuji, I begin my own chant.

> *Climb these stone steps*
> *slowly, slowly—rain tapping*
> *on the old snail shell.*

We eat a vegetarian Zen lunch that I think would have pleased Basho: triangles of black rice, wasabi potatoes, fresh lettuce garnished with slices of red and yellow pepper, blackberry pickled onion, black rice soup, and noodles made from ancient rice called Kodaimai. The simplicity and elegance of the meal are mirrored in our surroundings.

> *Pale yellow orchid*
> *in a tangerine pot—rain*
> *pooling in the pond.*

Back at the youth hostel in the evening, I enjoy the hot bath, savoring the sweetness of the day and anticipating the next day's trip to Matsushima.

> *Cedar wood cradling*
> *this body, steamy water dreams:*
> *island in the mist.*

JULY 10, 2009

Our day begins with a visit to a small Shinto shrine, Okama Jinja, in the city of Shiogama, where the purification of salt is done each year. Shinto priests go out

on the bay to gather seaweed and sea water and boil them down until only salt remains. During an elaborate festival, which includes a parade through the streets, the salt is offered to the kami (Shinto gods).

We proceed to the many stairs leading to Shiogama Jinja, the large shrine on a hill overlooking the city. Here, music seems to emanate from the hill itself.

Wind brushing rain-wet
leaves—ghostly taiko drums
weaving through old pines.

29

In front of the shrine, freshly caught fish glisten in the sun, this morning's offering to the kami from local fishermen. The chanting of a Shinto ritual in progress draws me to a building where hundreds of pairs of shoes are lined up outside. People sit quietly, their eyes focused on priests in robes of deep blue, purple, and white, who move gracefully across a raised platform. All around us the air feels charged with energy.

Guttural pigeons
chatter on the pebbled ground—whoosh!
wings rushing skyward.

On the tallest pine
a silent crow shines—shrill flute
trailing in the wind.

In the museum is an Omikoshi, a float used in Shinto parades. The kami is believed to be inside this shining black and red lacquer carriage, which is decorated with gold cranes, swords, and mirrors. Periodically, the kami is given an outing, carried through the streets on the shoulders of men during a Matsuri, or Festival.

Outside once again, I imagine the kami embracing the eternal wind and sun that grace the hill.

Sweeping the sky clean—
the beat of joyful drumming
in crystal sunlight.

Our next stop is Matsushima, the island whose beauty left Basho unable to write a single poem. This island is also known as Koyasan of Tokohu, hallowed ground where many go to pray for safe passage to the Pure Land.

On the boat ride, we pass many intriguing islands, some arched like waves about to break, others shaped like animals or birds, and still others with open tunnels through which the wind echoes.

Passing by Turtle,
Crane and Whale, we follow singing
waves to sacred pines.

Upon our arrival, we are greeted by the gentle ringing of wind chimes and hot midday sun. I buy a white straw hat to protect the top of my head and walk to Zuiganji, a Rinzai Zen temple first built in 828 and most recently reconstructed in 1609. Basho, then, surely walked these same paths. A serene Jizo watches over the entrance, and the temple roofs seem to float among golden clouds.

In the main building constructed by the samurai Date Masamune, the walls are painted in startling shades of glowing gold, indigo, scarlet, and forest green. Hawks symbolizing the bravery of the Date clan keep watch in the skies, peacocks preen, and white herons flee from predator claws. Here the Sato brothers, Masamune and Tadamune, who killed themselves after the death of their lord, are laid in state. Here, too, the Meiji Emperor spent the night in 1876.

A woman sighs, whispers—
dried leaves skittering toward
lightness on the path.

In a nearby grove of trees are caves once used for meditation by Zen monks. Today, they hold their ashes, some dating as far back as 1192.

A tiny red Shinto shrine on a steep hillside catches my eye.

Red shining beneath
a sunlit roof of maples—listen!
Crow call bound for home.

Is it true that there is a set amount of energy in the universe, which is continually transformed? If so, where is the energy that once comprised these ancient figures? And where will the energy of which we are made eventually go?

Wind chimes sound once again, and as I leave, shadows quiver over the stone path.

JULY 11, 2009

This afternoon the Taki Haiku Group of Sendai gives us a kukai demonstration. For this poetry competition, the members pass around and rate the haiku they've written, thirty-three in all. Then the kukai master shares the ratings and comments on each poem. If I were able to speak Japanese, I would love this session, but as it is, I don't understand a word, and we have no translators. So I occupy myself by observing individual members of the Haiku Group. I am especially taken by the elegant woman directly across from me. She is dressed in a tan blouse and pale green jacket accented with a red necklace, earrings, lipstick, and eyeglass frames, all perfectly balanced against her dark complexion and black hair. She seems to me a work of art. I wonder about her husband, her family, whether she has a job, what she's thinking …

Despite my inability to fully understand the words, I appreciate our hosts' generosity. At the end of the session, they give each of us a beautiful calligraphy version of a haiku and stalks of fresh lavender. I weave the lavender into the corded band of my Matsushima hat.

As we head for the train, I look one last time at the high-rise buildings of this multifaceted city.

> *Who has given these*
> *concrete hives wings to lift them*
> *from such busy streets?*

I settle in for yet another long ride, the sharp scent of lavender wafting around me.

> *Journal pages still*
> *damp with yesterday's*
> *rain—Sendai's parting gift.*

JULY 12, 2009

Hiraizumi, 5:45 A.M.

> *Just before dawn—*
> *chattering voices chasing*
> *the waning moon.*

Across the street a woman wearing a straw hat, black rubber gloves that reach to her elbows, black boots up to her knees, and a blue-patterned shirt and pants, is talking and gesturing to a woman from the ryokan, who laughs in response. This scene quickly merges in my mind with early morning walks in the village of Huangcun, China. Think of all the women in all the villages around the world, how they wake from their dreams and reenter the world each day through chatter and work.

7:00 A.M. Chimes sound from the village, and the scent of fish and onions cooking wafts up from the kitchen. 7:17 A.M. I am wandering without clear direction in my reading of Basho's journal. Forward and back, not quite up to Hiraizumi, still thinking of Matsushima. Basho reports that he lodged at an inn there, watching moonlight glittering on the bay and listening to the roaring winds. How I would like to have stayed a night on Matsushima and seen that same moon.

After breakfast, wearing my Matsushima hat, I trail behind the group as we walk through the village. We are in search of history, but I am focused on the old man harvesting potatoes and the woman cutting cabbage, on birdsong in the fields and the magenta phlox that makes me long for home. So many generations of birds, cicadas, and butterflies have passed through these fields. So many people have cultivated them.

Sweet onion stalks—how
many years have these bodies
bowed to summer's heat?

Several signs on buildings say "Refuge Center," and at the museum, we learn that this valley town, ringed by mountains and built beside a river, is prone to flooding and earthquakes. The most recent earthquake was in 1949, the year of my birth. I imagine my own mother giving birth to me and wonder what children were born here in the year of the earthquake. Where are they now? In a museum in Morocco, I once saw the photograph of a pregnant woman taken in 1949 and wondered about the path her child's life had taken. Would our paths ever cross? How strange to think of all the women of the world who were born in 1949, of all the mothers giving birth.

Finding a plate on display that we are allowed to touch, I run my fingers over its worn surface, enjoying the coolness of the old clay.

Nine centuries—curved
lines pooling around one square
in this shallow plate.

I am keenly aware of the people living in the valley and the history that towers over them as we head toward the site of Benkei's and Yoshitsune's deaths in 1189.

Climbing the steps, layer
upon layer of years pressed
beneath our tired feet.

Bracelet of clover
woven in the fields below
graces an old stone.

Basho writes that he was moved to tears at the site of Yoshitsune's death: "When a country is defeated, there remain only mountains and rivers and on a ruined castle in spring only grasses thrive." (Yuasa, 118) He quickly follows this with a passage about "the wonders of Chuson Temple" and the glow of its gold chapel, which is our next stop.

On our trek up to Chuson-ji, we pass one souvenir shop after another, each with glittering charms, prayer plaques, and fluttering banners. Sunday visitors swarm the paths, and it's difficult to feel any spirituality here. All the glitter and even the gold in the chapel leave me untouched, but I am moved by the scent of lilies at the foot of a guardian Jizo, by the lotus blooming in the pond, and by the hint of lavender on my Matsushima hat, to which I have added a pink wildflower from the field below.

By midafternoon, exhausted from walking and feeling filled to the brim with sensations, I almost skip Motsuji Temple and Jodo, the Heian gardens begun by Lord Fujiwara-no-Motohira at the very edge of the "civilized world" in 1105. However, the entire complex was meant to re-create Buddhism's Western Paradise on earth, and because of that enticing description, I rally. Walking the grounds, I thoroughly enjoy the iris gardens, the reflecting pond complete with islands and dragons, and the stream where a Floating Poetry Festival took place in 1986 to commemorate the 800th anniversary of the death of the third Fujiwara Lord Hidehira.

> *Wandering the stream's*
> *edge—bellflowers and hosta*
> *waiting to set sail.*

JULY 14, 2009

Time to move on again. I spend my last few moments at Osawa Onsen Ryokan looking out at the garden.

> *Open shoji—*
> *pink rhododendron resting*
> *beside turning maples.*

A gentle rain returns, and I leave the ryokan, dreaming of scarlet leaves in autumn.

We travel a little south and west, arriving at Naruko Onsen Station at 10:05, where we are greeted by three men dressed in traditional mountain garb: coats and hats made of woven rice grass, split-toed white socks called tabi, and straw sandals.

Oba-san, a tiny, wiry man of eighty-two, appears to be the leader, and his two companions, both muscular

and much younger, defer to him with great respect as they communicate with us. We are headed for a hike past the Shitomae Barrier and into the Dewa Sanzan area. At first, we think it just a coincidence that these three are planning to do the same. Eventually, we learn that they have heard of our trip (probably through the Okunohosomichi Network) and have volunteered to guide us on our two days of hiking here. Unfortunately, the weather is not cooperating.

Shitomae rains—
even the crescent lantern
has surrendered its light.

Nevertheless, we persist in sloshing our way through the town, following a largely overgrown path through the Tori gate beyond the remains of the Barrier, and then climbing up the steps to a small mountain shrine. It is so dark under the trees that I am unable to capture an image with my camera. Oba-san does not join us on the rest of the hike, but waves his good wishes to us and his two companions as he is whisked away in a white van.

Shoes squishing with mud and rain, we head for Naruko Gorge, walking past an abandoned ski area where the clock has stopped at 7:45 for what could be eternity. The mists swirl around the mountaintops and we follow these men deeper and deeper into the mountains.

Swift waters stirring
river mud, sulfur mists:
deep mountain breathing.

Unable to see what's above us, I focus on the trail, collecting leaves, a walnut shell, and seed pods, and watching every step to avoid falling on the slick trail.

Gore-Tex boots—slow steps
slipping behind straw sandals:
weaving mountain path.

Past Ofukugawa (Big Deep Creek) and Kofukugawa (Small Deep Creek), we come to a clearing where the sun briefly breaks through the clouds, allowing us to look back at Flower Creek Mountain Gorge.

Amid the shining
mulberries, cuckoos calling—
summer ripeness.

But the kami have not finished with the rain, and we are soon blessed with another shower. We stop at an almost empty restaurant where we enjoy hot noodles and green tea. When we step outside again, the rain has stopped, but the winds are fierce. We walk back down through the town, our plastic raincoats flapping behind us, and turn onto a narrow path that leads into the mountains. Many Yama Jinja, small mountain temples, are tucked under the trees where people come to make offerings to the kami, asking for the favor of fertility or good fortune. Our guides share local stories about dangers in the forest, pointing out a marker where it is said that some who were brave enough withstood the powers of evil together by sleeping on the spot overnight.

Wind, wind, wind! And darkness
beneath the tussled trees—kami
welcome or warning?

Finally, after climbing up and down the mountain paths and fording a stream, we arrive at the Gatekeeper's Hut, the original building where Basho himself found shelter, although he complained about being kept awake by a horse pissing very close to his bed. We, however, are welcomed by the scent of cedar smoke and a crackling fire that warms our feet. We have "miles to go before we sleep," but this stopping place feels wonderful.

JULY 15, 2009

7:00 A.M. Chimes in the mountain village and then, over the loudspeaker, "Ohayo gozaimasu" plus many words I don't understand. An old man shuffles down the road outside my window.

We are treated to a full Japanese breakfast with fresh fish caught in a nearby stream and vegetables from local gardens. Oba-san has sent cabbage from his own garden especially for us.

Planting cabbage seeds
in spring, could he know we would
come in time to taste?

We visit a local elementary school. A newspaper reporter is on hand to record the event as students read their haiku to us, and we share translations of ours with them. Oba-san grins and recites his own, which goes something like this:

Watching
the morning glories, my tea
tastes better.

The group ends by singing the school song, and Oba-san proudly joins in.

Joyful, joyful song—
thin neck stretched, vocal chords tight:
this small summer bird!

I witness in Oba-san the deep spirituality that can be found in everyday life, which is the heart of *wabi sabi*. He gives us a tour of a traditional teahouse, leading us through a very small doorway that opens our minds and hearts to the beauty of what is simple and ordinary (*wabi*) and to the bittersweet serenity of loneliness and awareness of the passage of time (*sabi*).

Clear water trickles
over stone—a cricket sings
in the empty room.

Coming out into the light, we set off for Natagiri Pass.

> *Overhead, hawks circling*
> *in blue sky—potato harvest*
> *beneath our feet.*

Oba-san is in the lead, his body bouncing with energy as he chatters with the Japanese speakers in our group. At the top of Natagiri Pass, which literally means "sharp sword," Oba-san stands beside a stone tablet engraved with a Basho poem and sings.

> *Thin finger traces*
> *the old poet's words: trembling*
> *voices shine from the stone.*

Beneath the stone is an offering of safflowers beginning to wilt. Who will be singing Oba-san's songs fifty years from now?

That night I learn Oba-san's life story: how he was a village farmer all his life except for the years of the War when he served in the military, how he cared for his wife during the 108 days she was dying of cancer, how he honored her with poetry at her funeral, how he journals and writes in calligraphy every day. Basho wrote

that at Obanazawa he found the unchanging within the changing. I have found it at Akakura Onsen, where Oba-san is passing on his knowledge while living each day fully and joyfully. I wonder what Oba-san would think of this Nanao Sakaki poem that I love:

If you have time to chatter
Read books
If you have time to read
Walk into mountain, desert, and ocean
If you have time to walk
sing songs and dance
If you have time to dance
Sit quietly, you Happy Lucky Idiot.

(Sakaki, 33)

I think I can see him smiling and nodding his head.

JULY 15, 2009

Oba-san comes to say good-bye. He is dressed in casual Western-style pants and shirt, and around his head he wears a white bandana with red designs. He brings gifts for Professor Rodd, the leader of our group, and a poem by Yoshi (his pen name):

The flowers are supported by the branches
The branches are supported by the trunk
The trunk is supported by the roots
But the roots are invisible.

In the flurry of our departure, I watch Oba-san standing alone and to the side. I imagine him tomorrow morning alone in his garden. He has given us so much. What have we left behind with him? How many more springs and summers will he spend in his garden?

Behind us, mountains
diminish and fade—still light
glistens on the grass.

At one of the first train stops, one of Oba-san's companions leaps onto the train, ninja-style, with a bag full of small straw sandals laced in green. Attached to each is a poem in calligraphy—Oba-san's parting gift for each of us. I can see him picturing the delivery and smiling to himself.

As the train carries us southeast to Obanazawa and Yamagata, it follows the river that narrows behind us and finally disappears, the train's whistle echoing in the dark tunnel we have entered. I sing to myself the refrain of a favorite song "Turning Toward the Morning," by Gordon Bok:

Oh, my Joanie, don't you know
That the stars are swinging slow,
And the seas are rolling easy
As they did so long ago?
If I had a thing to give you,
I would tell you one more time
That the world is always turning
toward the morning.

(Turning Toward the Morning (c) 1975, Gordon Bok, BMI)

I think Oba-san would approve of this as well.

In Obanazawa, we meet a Basho scholar who leads us through the museum, explaining how Basho spent his time here visiting his friend Seifu, who was a trader in safflowers. He quotes Basho's most famous poem:

an old pond
a frog jumps in
sound of water.

(as translated by Rodd)

He tells us that if your spirit isn't calm, you don't hear the sound of the water. My mind wanders, thinking about the deepening layers of this trip and the sound of its water. My eyes are drawn to a calligraphy scroll. A companion

kindly translates for me: *building where the moonlight remains.* Ah! My mind returns to thoughts of Oba-san in the mountains.

Even the strongest
cedar yields to the falling
snow—winter dreams.

Cool breeze from distant
Gassan—hollyhock petals
flutter in hot sun.

Time to think about the upcoming days of this journey: Yamagata, where my homestay family—Mr. Takahashi, his wife, son, daughter-in-law, and two grandsons—await, and the Dewa Sanzan where the sacred mountains lie.

Last evening is a blur of incongruous images: a symposium at Yamagata University, followed by a reception; Takahashi-san meeting and taking me to his home; an after-dinner trip to the supermarket with his wife Matsuka-san; the ride home under the stars with the convertible top down; the toilet lid in their bathroom that lifts automatically as I approach it; the feeling of sinking into my futon and falling immediately to sleep.

This morning we tour Takahashi-san's garden,

which must be experienced slowly…

each tiny section a little forest …

in which you can get lost, layer upon layer…

like Takahashi-san himself, whose gruff exterior

falls away, little by little…

Next stop, a day trip to Yamedera about which Basho said:

> The whole mountain was made of massive rocks
> thrown together and covered with age old pines
> and oaks. The stony ground itself bore the color of
> eternity, paved with velvety moss. The doors of the
> shrines built on the rocks were firmly barred and
> there was not a sound to be heard. As I moved on
> all fours from rock to rock, bowing reverentially at
> each shrine, I felt the purifying power of this holy
> environment pervading my whole being.

> > In the utter silence
> > of a temple,
> > a cicada's voice alone
> > penetrates the rocks.
> >
> > (as translated in Yuasa, 122-123)

Some have said that Basho's cicada might be a reference to Todo Yoshitada, a close friend in Basho's youth with whom Basho wrote poetry and who died suddenly at the age of twenty-five.

It is not surprising to me that the mountain would have this effect on Basho, for although it is not known as the mountain of death (like Gassan), it *feels* like the mountain of death. The mountainside is pocked with caves where Tendai monks starved themselves to death in meditation. Thousands of wooden memorial markers are tucked next to small shrines along the path, and there are many stone grave markers with fresh flowers, food, candle and incense offerings as well as Jizo and stone lanterns along the way.

Spinning the wheel on the the wooden memorial markers symbolizes a recitation of all the Buddhist sutras, either for one who has died or for yourself. Am I a believer? I'm not sure, but Daoism and Buddhism in their simplest forms make sense to me. Thinking of the energy flow of the universe and following The Way, I spin once each for my mother and father, and once for myself for good measure.

> *Whir of the worn wheel*
> *weaves with birdsong—insects crawl*
> *through the rotting grain.*

Approaching the Hall of Amida Buddha, I read: "Clap your hands together and make today a day of gratitude." A serendipitous echo of the quote on the front of the "Crystal Mind" notebook I have recently purchased: "Every morning when I wake up, I treasure the innocence of being able to enjoy each day."

Finally I reach the top of the mountain.

White butterflies
brushing stone Buddhas—open
doors leading westward.

The clacking sound of wood against wood fills the air. Several monks demonstrate how to use these wooden balls attached by string to wooden sticks for walking meditation.

My companion repeats a meditation chant she learned from a Zen Master: "Clear mind, clear mind, clear mind, don't know." I peer through a stand of bamboo, my eyes drawn to shining red roofs in the village far below. What must it be like to live in the shadow of this mountain? I am reminded of the Hanging Monastery I visited in China, which is literally built into the mountainside and rests on huge posts sunk deep into the rock. Both places settle within me, radiating peace, well-being, and an unnameable yet pleasant sadness. Perhaps this is *sabi*?

After lunch with my companions, I opt for a solitary descent from the mountain. The trail seems surprisingly unfamiliar. Is it me or the world that has been transformed? The immensity of the ancient trees and rocks is overwhelming, and I see for the first time long vines hanging down over the rock face a hundred feet above my head. *Cluck-cluck-cluck. Cree-cree. Caw ca-aw ca-aw c-aw.* The insistent crows in the treetops chant endlessly.

I follow hidden side paths where pilgrims have placed a teddy bear, a small stuffed Jizo, a wooden toy. Can there be so many lost children? The path continues down through blue hydrangeas and lacy ferns. I am startled by a moss-covered rock with small trees growing out of it. It looks just like Takahashi-san's miniatures—amazing how his small garden created the feeling of an entire forest as I walked on its carefully placed stones.

Farther down the path, a soft trickle of water flows from a rock, and beside it, one tree looms, solemn and silent, a sentinel that Basho surely passed as he climbed this very mountain. And yes, the whine of cicadas penetrates the air. All other visitors have, for the moment, vanished, and I hold my breath, wanting to savor this emptiness just a little longer.

Footsteps approaching
from above—shadows passing
over the still ferns.

I place a stone in the soft moss growing at the base of a stone monument and move on, reminded of Mark Strand's poem "Keeping Things Whole"—the way our bodies displace the air wherever we are, and how the air moves in behind us, filling the space we once occupied. (Strand, 40)

Beside the path, a polished black marble stone with white flecks gleams in the sunlight filtering through the tree branches. A freshly cut and painted wooden marker rests against it, in front of it a candle and a white cup with a black lotus design.

Drop of wax hugging
the slender candle—whose breath
blew out the flame?

I walk through the sleepy town and buy four hand-carved and painted Daruma from a local craftsman. It is only later that I learn that the Daruma represent the Bodhidharma, who was said to have meditated so long that he lost both of his legs.

The train rumbles into the station and we board, leaving behind the high-pitched whine of Basho's cicadas and the soft wind in the pines.

Back in Yamagata, I meet up with Takahashi-san, and we return to his home, where Matsuka-san and their two grandsons, Tomiki and Matsuki, are waiting to go to the new sushi bar for dinner. In the car the boys put in a CD of English songs, and we sing together: *B-I-N-G-O, B-I-*

N-G-O, AND BINGO WAS HIS NAME-OH, and *HEAD, SHOULDERS, KNEES, AND TOES—KNEES AND TOES—* smiling and laughing all the way. Tomiki and Matsuki cannot contain their excitement in the sushi bar, as they use the touch screen to order dish after dish for all of us. By the end of the meal, each has piled at least eight dishes in front of him, compared to my four, and I am stuffed. Matsuka-san and Takahashi-san smile indulgently.

At home, I admire the ancestor portraits and the shining gold-and-black lacquered Butsudan, which belonged to Takahashi-san's parents. His family is descended from the upper class, perhaps even the samurai or wealthy merchants of the Tokugawa period.

He points out the family crest that graces not only the Butsudan, but also the overhead lights throughout the house and a framed piece of art in the genkan.

After cake and tea, we exchange gifts. I am delighted to receive a red tablecloth with stylized blue flowers, which will remind me of this homestay each time I use it. I think again about the mysterious layers beneath the surface of this family and accept that there is much I will never know.

Drifting off to sleep
mother and father keep watch—
frogs croak in the garden.

As we head for Haguro, I am reading *Awesome Nightfall: The Life, Times, and Poetry of Saigyo*, William LaFleur, author and translator. I am moved to copy poem after poem into my journal and begin to understand why Basho held Saigyo in such high esteem. His poems are elegant, crystal clear, deeply resonant, and wise. I have found a new friend.

> Shaking the bell
> on this mountain, am I loosened from
> this world now?
> Can I shake myself enough
> to know what lies ahead for me?
>
> (as translated in LaFleur, 19)

I ask the same question of myself.

We settle ourselves into a communal space in the temple on Haguro, one room for the men and one for the women. Our view looks out over the mountains and trees. The sunlight glittering on the leaves pulls me out to explore the temple area. Who knows how long the sunlight will last during this rainy season?

Haguro is part of the Dewa Sanzan, one of the mountain areas most sacred to the Yamabushi who practice Shugendo, a fusion of esoteric Buddhism (Shingon and Tendai) and Shinto beliefs and practices. Haguro is also known as Black Feather or Black Wing Mountain and is symbolic of birth for the pilgrims who hike it. Prince Hachiko is said to have opened this area for religious practice in the ninth century, and it is still a magnet for pilgrims today. Banners fluttering around a large open area near the temple and people dressed in pilgrimage white tell us the pilgrimage season is gearing up.

At the main temple, a priest and three assistants dressed in elegant long white robes are conducting a service. Their chanting is punctuated by the clatter of coins

servers in white with large black hats on their heads float by like ghosts, and then the clack of a wooden instrument breaks the silence. Now another female chant begins accompanied by a high-pitched wind instrument and a stringed instrument of some kind. All this takes place in front of a large mirror set in black lacquered wood.

Next a priest with a long red train trailing behind him begins a graceful dance, waving a large, leafy branch with a white and red cloth attached to it. A woman in a red-and-gold robe, with a row of tiny mirrors dangling across her forehead, enters and dances silently, seeming to be in rhythm with the croaking frog. Suddenly a large number of people in ordinary dress enter, a shade is quickly lowered, and loud drumming and the shaking of bells begin. I am once again reminded of the Latin Catholic masses of my childhood, where I was mesmerized by the incomprehensible pageantry of priest and altar boys, the ringing of bells, chanting and choir music, and the raising of a glittering gold chalice.

hitting against the side of a wooden box, the high-pitched squeal of a flute, and the croaking of a frog in Mirror Lake behind us. Women dressed in scarlet robes with white tops come and go across the "stage" area. They raise and lower their arms in unison, gently ringing golden bells in their hands. Long purple, green, gold, and red sashes trail down from their wrists to the tatami mat under their feet. They turn to reveal shining mirrors on their foreheads, then exit holding open fans above their heads. Three male

Wandering behind a smaller temple, I stumble on a row of pinwheels gently turning in the wind.

Pinwheels squeak, swish, squeak—
chatter of children floating
on the summer breeze.

They lead to a cemetery of sorts where every manner of Jizo is dressed in an amazing array of clothing that seems to represent the dead: a favorite black-and-white running jacket, an aqua-and-yellow child's backpack, a faded Vantage 1960s ball cap, a sleeveless gray T-shirt, a fur-lined winter jacket, a flowered Hawaiian shirt. I am haunted by the thought of so many people sending their loved ones to another world.

On Haguro-san
whine of cicadas—ancient
songs forever rising.

From the pond comes the croak of a single frog, as dissonant as the clacking of instruments in the shrine. I notice the footwear placed at the feet of the Jizo: woven straw sandals, Nike sneakers, a worn pair of pink slippers. Again the *cla-a-a-c-c-k, cl-a-a-a-c-c-k* of the frog.

The temple grounds have closed, and I am completely alone watching afternoon shadows fall over the scarlet steps of the temple. I walk past a row of smaller shrines and come to a larger-than-life statue of Basho. Held captive by the hush of this place, which is interrupted only by the insistent chant of cicadas among pines and cedars, I can almost feel his spirit flowing. Reluctantly, I return to the temple to rejoin the others, thinking about a quote by Saigyo: "Pledges are best when made on precipices above it all." (LaFleur, 40) What pledges might be mine to make on this journey through the Dewa Sanzan?

Tonight I present to the group my thoughts about an article by Thomas Heyde entitled "Basho and the Aesthetics of Wandering." I have read this article three times, but it is only now that I determine the heart of it for me. The first point is that wandering is like dance, each person creating a particular rhythm in response to physical, spiritual, and psychological surroundings. This gives me an entirely new sense of my traveling companions, as I imagine each of us creating our own free-spirited dance that will eventually become the choreography of our shared journey. Although we can be aware of only a small part of each person's dance, what each contributes enriches our experience. The second point that strikes me is the following quote: "For a person who has the spirit, everything he sees becomes a flower, and everything he imagines turns into a moon." (4) This is a thought that I want to weave together with ideas in Mary Oliver's poem, "The Swan," about the necessity of understanding the world through the imagination and honoring it with our actions. (Oliver, 17)

The third important point in Heyde's article for me is his description of Basho's experience at Gassan: "… the mountain environment left a trace on his body and mind, and he, likewise, left a trace on the mountain …"(7) What traces are we each taking with us and leaving behind? Fourth is this quote: "… because the event of coming to know a place is ephemeral for the wanderer…the time actually spent…becomes more valuable and the experience of engagement more poignant …" (8) Here, perhaps, is my mountain precipice pledge: to be as actively engaged as possible in this experience so I can later affirm the reality of it. And finally, lest I become too focused on holding on to what I can never keep, this quote: "… in wandering we enter the flow of the Universe." (9) And to enter the flow, I must be willing to let go—the other half of my mountain pledge.

July 18, 2009

This morning I am awake early and again feel compelled to wander the grounds of Haguro-san alone. I walk past two of my companions who are sitting on the steps, equally absorbed in their own thoughts. We nod, giving each other the space we need to enter the day. The rain begins slowly as I walk back to the Jizos. Like the ones in Nikko, they seem to exert an emotional pull on me. Someone has risen before me and lit three incense sticks and two candles. Smoke wafts into the air, mixing with the rain that is now pouring down and sliding in sheets from the shining rooftops to land and bounce up from the pebbled ground. I light two candles for my parents and wonder how long these candles will burn. How will the energy released from them join with all the energies of the universe?

Candles flickering
beside lit incense—footsteps
in the morning rain.

I wander among the Jizo, looking closely again.

Faded tan cap rests
on weathered stone—empty hands
pressed palm to palm.

Bright yellow sandals
tipped against stone—spidery
Kanji brushing the sole.

Grateful for the rain that has silenced us all, I walk back to our temple shelter on the wet stones that, like the ones in Takahashi-san's garden, seem carefully placed to slow my steps.

After breakfast, we separate into small groups to explore Haguro-san in our own ways. On this mountain which symbolizes birth, we are readying ourselves for the long hike up Gassan and Yudono, mountains symbolizing death and rebirth respectively. In spite of the rain, my group decides to walk down the 2,441 steps at a leisurely pace, stopping to touch the wet cedar trunks, pale green moss, and curls of thin bark. We search out the site of a hut where Basho once stayed.

In the old pond
a moss-covered stone—sweet wild
lily scents the path.

We return to the path, protected by the sacred cedars that have guarded the mountain for centuries.

By the rushing stream
an orange leaf falls—mushrooms
sprouting in the darkness.

In the village at the foot of the mountain, we meet up with the rest of our companions. One, who often seems like a Jizo herself, points out a pale green Jizo in which incense can be burned. I quickly purchase it. She smiles and laughs, saying, "In winter, don't forget: make a Jizo with snow, take a picture, and send to me." As the snow begins to fall in Maine, I will remember.

After lunch, we wander through a museum where I collect quotes about the importance of the pilgrimage in Dewa Sanzan:

> Going around the three mountains, the pilgrims travel symbolically through the whole world: present, past, and future, all the while maintaining their existence.

> After going through the three mountains, the pilgrims have been born again and come back to this world with purified bodies and strong spirits.

> By contemplating phenomena in nature that change with the seasons, one penetrates their underlying eternity, perceiving them as unchangeable, and concludes with the idea that the changes blend together into one.

Before sleep—sacred
conch echoes from tree to tree
on the mountain slope.

July 19, 2009

This morning I rise with great anticipation. This is the day we are meant to climb Gassan and then Yudono, also known as Moon and Hot Springs mountains respectively. Before we board the bus, I read a little Saigyo:

> Following the paths
> the gods passed over, I seek
> their innermost place;

56

up and up to the highest of all:
peak where wind soughs through the pines.

(as translated in LaFleur, 50)

At the foot of the mountain, the clouds seem to be breaking up, and we even see a patch of blue sky. However, as the bus climbs to the station where we are to begin our hike, the clouds thicken, the wind picks up, and the rain begins again. By the time we dress ourselves in plastic raincoats and venture out onto the mountain, the wind is blowing so hard we can't stand up on the trail, even holding onto the thick green rope strung along the path to help us. The guide waves us back. Clearly, the mountain does not want to yield its secrets today.

> *Holding clouds close*
> *to the heart: not now, not now—*
> *secret kami meeting!*

In the small mountain shelter, we are joined by several other pilgrims forced to give up their dream. Among them are two elderly women who hardly seem dressed or rugged enough for such a strenuous hike, and yet their family tells us they have come especially to make the pilgrimage. The family hovers around them, worried that their health has been compromised by being out in such bad weather. Sadly, they may never have another chance at this pilgrimage.

On the way down, the bus horn penetrates the thick fog. The grasses and even the leaves of bushes are bent to the ground by the wind. The bus stops, as if the wind is pushing us back up the mountain, but the guide has made his final decision, and we must abide by it.

After lunch, I settle down in my room with *Awesome Nightfall*. I am sucked into Saigyo's poems with a force I haven't felt in years, as if this reading and not the hike over Gassan is meant to be my experience of death and rebirth. Each poem speaks to me more strongly than the last, until I finally give up any other thought except to read straight through to the end. Saigiyo's religious beliefs clarify much of what I've seen at the temples and shrines. He believed that the kami are manifestations of the buddhas and bodhisattvas, and that to worship Amaterasu, the Shinto Goddess of the Sun, is to pay respects simultaneously to Dainichi Nyorai, the buddha who taught the truth of esoteric Buddhism. Thus, Saigyo joined the two religions of Japan into one.

Since the Shinto kami are indeed manifestations of buddhahood and, since such kami are somehow present within all natural phenomena that impress us humans with their beauty and sacredness, then there need be no contradiction between even our most intense feelings for such things and efforts to move along the Buddhist path. Natural beauty is itself an articulation of the enlightened state. (LaFleur, 55)

According to LaFleur, waka poems were for Saigyo "a form of Buddhist mantra" (53), and yet Saigyo himself said:

> "As for the writing of verses, it is nothing more than the composition of a mere thirty-one syllables when one is emotionally stirred by the sight of blossoms or the moon; I know nothing about 'depths' in the composition of poetry."
>
> (as translated and quoted in LaFleur, 62)

His humility appeals to me, and I am moved by his use of the full moon as a focal point for extended meditation in which the mind/heart is progressively filled with light. In my mind I hear Debussy's "Clair de Lune," Beethoven's *Moonlight Sonata*, Paul Sullivan's "Full Moon Rising," their sounds filling me with light. I think of the mesmerizing light of the moon on winter snow or the rippling waves of Penobscot Bay. Saigyo's words sink deeper inside me.

> Clouds thickly mantle
> these mountains, but the blocked moon
> had already taken up residence
> in my mind, so nothing now prevents
> me from seeing its serenity there.
>
> (as translated in LaFleur, 66-67)

I look at the rain now blown sideways by the wind. How fitting this poem is for today's experience of Gassan! In fact, everything about this day seems serendipitous. Of his own death, Saigyo writes:

> Let it be spring
> and under cherry blossoms that
> I die, while the moon
> is perfect at mid month,
> like it was for his peaceful passing.
>
> (as translated in LaFleur, 69)

What poem might I write for my own death? What poem would my mother have written for herself?

> Journeying alone:
> now my body knows the absence
> even of its own heart,

which stayed behind that day when
it saw Yoshino's steps.

> (as translated in LaFleur, 76)

I read poem after poem, and each one seems to be written directly to me. There is even one that seems to describe how his own poems have come to me today:

Early summer rains:
no let up, no glimpse of sky,
but somewhere inside
this thick bank of clouds a crying
mountain warbler threads its way.

> (as translated in LaFleur, 83)

I give thanks to the kami for these rains that have halted our journey and to Basho for introducing me to Saigyo and sending me on this path of purposeful wandering.

*Yudono-san—ghosts
on the winding path: rising
mist calling the sun.*

We make an early morning visit to Yudono-san Jinja. In this year of the ox, we are greeted by two ox statues. Is it especially auspicious for a person born in the year of the ox to be visiting this sacred place in the year of the ox? I'd like to think it is. The tinkling of the bell on my backpack reminds me of the Yamabushi protection amulet I attached to it yesterday.

Just before entering the shrine, we remove our shoes, everyone's feet now somehow equal and vulnerable as we step on the cold stones. We bow, receive purification, and enter the heart of the shrine area where water that surfaces from the heart of the mountain flows over the rock face of a hill.

Bare feet on warm stone,
sweet sake, crisp lettuce leaves—
today's breakfast!

As we leave, two birds cross the valley. Their song and the gushing of the mountain stream fill me with joy as the sun finds an opening in the clouds.

After breakfast we are off again, to Churenji, where we see the self-mummified saint Tetsumonkai displayed in a glass case. According to legend, after killing two samurai by mistake, Tetsumonkai fled to Yudono-san and hid in a cave. A spider spun a web at the entrance, which he saw as a sign that he should become a monk. During his lifetime, he traveled to Tokyo and gave his left eye to cure all those who suffered with a terrible eye disease. He is also said to have built bridges and cured plagues. At age 62, he chose to mummify himself so that his body could remain in this world and help others. In order to do this, he gradually gave up eating—first grains and beans, then all vegetables raised by humans—consuming only tree bark, fruits of trees, nuts, and grasses. Eventually, all flesh and fat were gone, leaving only skin and bones. Then he drank lacquer to "take care of the intestines." At the very end, he entered a pine box set two feet into the ground with a bamboo pipe for air and a bell. When the bell stopped ringing when people called down the bamboo pipe, they knew he was dead. After 1000 days, the body was removed to be memorialized and lacquered. His body rests in this shrine, where every twelve years his clothing is changed. (And yes, it is this year, the year of the ox, in which this occurs!) I can't stop staring into the case.

Prayer beads dangling
from his lacquered palm—do they
still tremble with life?

Yet another "year of the ox" phenomenon occurs at this shrine. This is the one day every twelve years that the public can walk behind a special curtain, usually only allowed to the priests. What am I to make of these twelve-year cycles, five of them since the year I was born?

Next stop is the Mogami River, where we travel by boat. Like Basho, we have high waters due to recent heavy rains. Our guide is a "Mogami River Man Extraordinaire." He owns the boat service and a coffee shop across the river, has written a novel based on Basho's supposed experience with coffee, and has a CD of river songs. He serves us a lunch of stew and soba noodles on the boat, then serenades us:

I'm going down to Sakata
Stay strong and healthy
Please don't catch your death.

You can make a crooked turnip
into a salty stew, but if it's too salty
I'll never get it down.

We are blessed with a light breeze, sunlight, brilliant shades of green all along the banks, and hydrangeas again in every hue of blue, pink, and purple. We disembark for a quick visit to the coffee shop beside a small Shinto shrine where both Yoshitsune and Basho are said to have stopped during their travels.

My mind wanders, imagining this place in other times, other seasons.

> *Under the green leaves,*
> *promise of scarlet turnings—*
> *swift flowing river.*

How can there be more to experience on this day? And yet there is. We board the bus again and head for Sakata on the western shore of Honshu. We tour the

Honma mansion, built by a wealthy merchant during the Tokugawa era. Sated with history and information, all I can do is float along behind the tour, trying to capture the images and sensations that put me back in touch with myself and the physical space I inhabit.

> *Old man clutching*
> *a crow's feather—wind rattles*
> *the sunlit shoji.*

> *Coolness—sweet scent*
> *of lilies, footsteps gracing*
> *the old tatami.*

A midmorning train takes us to Kisakata, which Basho contrasts with Matsushima. "Matsushima is a cheerful laughing beauty, while the charm of Kisakata is in the beauty of its weeping countenance." (Yuasa, 129) Our experience mirrors Basho's. The Japan Sea is gray, and there is fog in the distance. After passing lonely stretches of beach and rock, we arrive in this sleepy town where rain begins to fall. The peak of Mount Chokai is in clouds as it was for Basho, and so we never get to witness how it is shaped like Mount Fuji, the reason it is much revered.

Kisakata gray:
rooftops wet with rain, Chokai
quiet under clouds.

We walk around the Islands in the Field, which were islands in the bay during Basho's visit. In 1804, an earthquake lifted the ground and water drained out of the bay, leaving fertile land for the rice fields that now stretch out before us.

This once floating earth
now planted—tender roots
longing for the sky.

We climb the hill of what was once Noin Isle, where the priest and poet Noin was said to have lived for three years in the eleventh century. Two hundred years later, Saigyo, greatly influenced by Noin, traveled in his footsteps. Four hundred years later, Basho followed the footsteps of both. Now, over three hundred years later, we follow the footsteps of all three. Layer upon layer. Who came before Noin? Who will follow us? And what about the earth? Will it soon shift beneath us or erupt out of Mount Chokai? And the sea? Is it preparing to flood the land again? Who will remember these fields then?

We ride the train back to Sakata, and a small group of us spend the afternoon wandering the art museum and discover a wonderful exhibit of *wabi* pottery.

Next to the museum is the garden of a summer home belonging to the Honma family. Although the garden is much larger than Takahashi-san's, it has the same mesmerizing effect. I'm quickly lost in a large maze-like forest, then suddenly found again. Light rain patters in the pond, white lilies float on its surface, and late-blooming irises reflect from its banks. A koi leaps and joins several others in a pinwheel dance before quickly separating again.

Fishtail swaying
side to side—pale yellow leaf
floating in its wake.

A leisurely departure from Wakaba Ryokan allows time to reflect on my surroundings. I have been charmed by its lovely curves. In the dining room, mirrors with rounded tops reflect each other as well as a carefully placed carving of wood on a third wall that echoes their shapes. In the garden, a stone basin with a ladle resting on its edge complements a round stone lantern with a circular opening and carefully rounded bushes—echoing, echoing, echoing.

A surreptitious peacefulness surrounds us. I am reminded of Bruce Feiler's book *Learning to Bow*, which I read before my first trip to Japan in 2002. When he arrived here to teach, his principal said to him, "If Japan had a national shape, it would be the circle…We like round things…We want things to run smoothly with no sharp edges." (88) Wakaba Ryokan certainly illustrates that, and I carry its quiet calm with me as I leave.

Waiting outside the train station, I look up at the gray sky:

Hawk circles above
high-rise buildings— scree! scree! scree!
Looking for lost islands?

I resolve to sit by myself on the long train ride to Kanazawa, and, like the hawk, to find islands in my wandering journals to explore and develop. Still, I can't help looking out the window. The coast flies by as we pass through tunnel after tunnel, allowing only brief glimpses of beaches and houses piled right up against the sea, the hills behind them pushing at their backs. Small gardens are nestled against the dunes, and suddenly I long to bury my feet in beach sand. I think of the precarious balance a traveler must maintain between collecting experiences in the moment and reflecting before all is lost. Either way, something must be surrendered. Yet again, the wisdom of the Buddha surfaces. And serendipitously again, it seems, I borrow a book, *The Master Haiku Poet: Matsuo Basho* by Makoto Ueda, from a companion and begin reading. The words follow the flow of my own thoughts, deepening and broadening my understanding. In discussing the *sabi* (or loneliness) in Basho's poems, Makoto Ueda suggests that instead of dissolving his ego completely in nature, Basho wanted to exist in the ordinary world and remain at peace. (66) His solution was "lightness," or *karumi*, an attitude of accepting all things as they come. Basho's concept of "loneliness," or *sabi*, is almost a "sublime feeling" that is deeper and beyond sadness. It is the blending of the temporal with the eternal, the joining of the infinitesimal and the infinite, which results in a feeling of communal loneliness. (52)

what solitude!
hanging from a nail—
a cricket
(as translated by Rodd)

I think of the spare paintings of Andrew Wyeth, which have always given me that same feeling of loneliness that goes beyond sadness and deepens into peace.

Ueda also concludes that in searching for how man should cope with the coldness of the universe, Basho looks to the way in which nature merely endures:

the first snow!
daffodil leaves bend
beneath the weight.
(as translated by Rodd)

Ah. My mind returns to Gordon Bok's song "Turning Toward the Morning," and its wisdom which has sustained me in difficult times. Still, maintaining this lightness and acceptance of all things is surely the task of a lifetime.

Ueda says that for Issa, a poet of the late eighteenth and early nineteenth century who was greatly influenced by Basho, poetry and life were inextricable, that his poetry was a record of his heart.(176) May my poems, too, be a diary of my heart.

We arrive at Kanazawa late in the afternoon and settle into Sumiyoshi-ya Ryokan, one of the oldest ryokan in the city. What will tomorrow's exploration bring?

We pass through Ishikawa Castle Gate, the only thing remaining of the castle which was destroyed in a fire in 1881.

Outside the castle walls, a hawk in silhouette gazes at the old moat.

Before we enter Kenrokuen Gardens, touted as one of the most beautiful gardens in Japan, one of my companions reads a list of "Six Attributes for Perfection of a Garden," which was developed during the Sung Dynasty in China: seclusion, spaciousness, artificiality, antiquity, abundant waters, and broad view potential. Kenrokuen was begun in the 1670s and, as it was gradually constructed over many years, strove to meet those attributes. However, once I enter the garden, all thoughts of perfection give way to simply experiencing the beauty and calm.

Tortoise Bridge, Flying
Geese—what's real? Today even
rain undecided.

We visit the Ishikawa Traditional Arts and Crafts Museum, where porcelain, lacquerware, gold leaf, metalwork, and cloth-dying are on display, and a group of women with a tour group chatter and ooh and ah, moving together like a flock of small birds, stopping now and then to gather around a scattering of grain. Their enthusiasm is contagious, and I follow behind, trying to see the exhibits through their eyes. Perhaps they have practiced some of these crafts themselves, giving them an insider's view of the skill each piece demonstrates.

Three of us spend a lazy afternoon meandering through the Noh Museum, some of the many city shops, and the old Samurai and Geisha districts of the city, imagining a livelier time when Tokugawa travelers and tradesmen walked these streets.

This morning I rise early and wander through the covered marketplace, breathing in the scent of fresh fish, vegetables, and fruits being unloaded from small trucks backed up to the entrances. Children in school uniforms, women and men in business suits, and country farmers pass through. How strange that long after I have left, they will continue to walk these streets, going about their lives in all seasons of the year.

I step out into the heat and bright light of the city streets and am assaulted by the fumes of buses and cars, and the hustle and bustle of this modern city. How far away the mountains of the Dewa Sanzan feel. I stop at Starbuck's for a café latte and open my journal to this Saigyo poem:

> Insect cries more faint
> in these clumps of autumn grass
> going dry: sympathy
> lent this field by shafts
> of the moon's light on it.
> (as translated in LaFleur, 85)

My mind is set adrift, and a gentle quiet spreads through me.

We board a late-morning train and spend much of the day crossing Honshu once more. Our destinations: Futaminoura and Ise on the eastern coast. I tunnel into my journals and notes, trying again to find the delicate balance between reflection and being in the moment.

> *Long-necked cranes searching*
> *ripe fields—bullet train slices*
> *through afternoon haze.*

Futaminoura seems to be a combination resort and pilgrimage town, its claim to fame being the sacred site of the Meoto Iwa ("wedded rocks"), which form a natural *tori* in the waters just off the beach. In summer, the sun

*In this sleepy town
the open mouths of sparrows—
shopkeeper's delight.*

rises between the two rocks. There is a small shrine and a plethora of shops at this end of the beach, but not many pilgrims or tourists this afternoon.

At the other end of the beach, our room at Iroha Ryokan looks out on the water. We can hear the waves breaking on the other side of a series of concrete steps leading up to a wall that protects these buildings from the ravages of ocean storms.

Three of us search for a shop selling "salty ice cream." As we enter, a swallow swoops inside, drawing our attention to the source of her interest nestled against the overhead light.

Next we wander down the concrete barrier and turn onto a quiet street that leads to Mishioden-jinja, a Shinto shrine given little attention in our description of Futaminoura sites. A sign tells us that salt crystals are collected from the sea and purified here, then offered to the kami, and that the poet Kamono Chomei wrote a waka here. We are enchanted by this deserted shrine hidden in the pines, but only later do we learn that salt purified here is offered twice each day to the Sun Goddess at Ise.

Caw! Caw! Thatched roof, closed
doors, steady beat of the sea—
step into darkness.

JULY 25, 2009

This is the last day of our Okunohosomichi journey, and we will be traveling to Ise, the holiest Shinto site in all of Japan. Technically, it was not part of Basho's journey, but on the last page of his journal he writes: "On September the sixth [after being home just a short while]…I left for the Ise Shrine, though fatigue of the long journey was still with me, for I wanted to see the dedication of a new shrine there." (Yuasa, 142) We, too, are tired, but feel the pull of Ise, the most appropriate place to end our pilgrimage into the heart of Japan.

I wake early and sit on the steps by the ocean, preparing myself for Ise. I open my journal and find a fitting Saigyo poem at the top of the page.

> Pounding waves are breakers …
> of my heart, so I spend the night
> in bed with the moon's
> light that slips through
> the gaps in my reed hut's roof.
>
> (as translated in LaFleur, 89)

Ever since that rainy day on Gassan, Saigyo has been weaving himself through the days of this journey, offering another way to enter the heart. I remove my shoes and put my feet in the water.

Plunk! Plash! Forward and back
yin yang, perfectly balanced
cleansing—new feet!

I turn the page to another Saigyo poem:

> Quiet mountain hut
> by a rice patch…till a deer's cry
> just outside startles me

70

and I move...so startling him:
we astonish one another!

(as translated in LaFleur, 92)

I am reminded of another early-morning rising years ago at Baxter State Park in Maine, where a doe and I faced each other at the pond's edge. Layer upon layer.

I look up to see that someone has entered the water, swimming a long, even crawl, and I envy him. Although I would dearly love to be immersed in these salty waters, I content myself with the waves intermittently reaching my toes. I could stay here forever, a feeling Saigyo knows well:

When fallen snow
buried the twigs bent by me
to mark a return trail,
unplanned, in strange mountains,
I was holed up all winter.

(as translated in LaFleur, 95)

It reminds me of my day lost in *Awesome Nightfall* and so many others when I have allowed myself to wander.

Snow has fallen on
field path and mountain paths,

burying them all,
and I can't tell here from there:
my journey in the midst of sky.

(Saigyo as translated in LaFleur, 96)

Will I feel this way when I sit out under the stars at home and think about Japan? Although I haven't yet left, I am already lonely for this place. *Jo, ha, kyu, zanshin—Zanshin—*"leaving behind the heart" (Kerr, 112). Is this another way of describing *sabi*? Is this how we enter "the very ebb and flow of the universe"? (Kerr 112)

I look down at my feet and think of how I have experienced this journey through my entire body, how it carries within it cool Pacific water, mossy paths, stone steps, beach sands, hot springs, fresh mountain vegetables, the scent of pine and blooming lilies.

The mind for truth
begins, like a stream, shallow
at first, but then
adds more and more depth
while gaining greater clarity.

(Saigyo as translated in LaFleur, 114)

Already anticipating the end of our journey together,

I return to the group, looking forward to what awaits us at Ise. Apparently, Ichihara-san, Director of the Okunohosomichi Network, has contacted his friend Nakamura-san, who, dressed as Basho, often accompanies groups like ours, and Nakamura-san has contacted *his* friend Yamamoto-san, president of the locally known Akafuku Sweets Company. Nakamura-san and Yamamoto-san appear at the ryokan in a company bus and guide us in grand style for the rest of a day that promises to be the hottest we've experienced since our arrival in Japan. We are very grateful for their generous sharing of knowledge and time, a delicious sashimi lunch, and afternoon treat of Akafuku tea and sweets, and the respite from walking, finding local transportation, and hauling luggage.

Ise Shrine is made up of two areas: the Outer Shrine, dedicated to the the deity of agriculture and commerce; and the Inner Shrine, dedicated to Amaterasu Omikami, the Sun Goddess. At the entrance to the Outer Shrine, a deafening cacophony of cicadas fills the air, which is oppressively hot and humid. After we pass through the untreated cypress tori, each column adorned by a simple branch of the sakaki with a white prayer paper tied to it, our footsteps crunch on the pebbled path that leads to the four fences that protect a thatched-roof building in which the deity is enshrined. Only the emperor is allowed to pass through the last fence to worship.

Sun on sacred leaves,
rhythmic chant deep in the trunks—
beckoning spirits.

For thirteen hundred years, the most sacred rituals of Shinto have been performed at Ise. Every twenty years, the shrines (over one hundred in all) are recreated by a little over six hundred craftsmen from around the country. It takes eight years for the entire process, and major festivals occur at each stage, the most important ones being the woodcutting, the carpentry, and the installation of the goddess. This process assures that the appearance of the

gods in this world remains pure, and that the craftsmen, who take twenty years to learn their craft, can pass on their knowledge to the next generation. In addition to reconstructing all buildings, people bring new stones from the area to replace the paths, and those most skilled in works of metal, lacquer, clay, and other precious materials from the earth recreate all of the gods' treasure found in the buildings. The next installation of the Sun Goddess will take place in 2014, and so preparations are already underway for the rebuilding.

Food and drink are offered to the Sun Goddess twice a day: water from the shrine area, salt purified at Mishioden-jinja (which we visited yesterday in Futaminoura), sake, rice, vegetables, fish and shellfish of the season, seaweed, and fruit.

The paths are dotted with many smaller shrines where pilgrims perform a specific ritual to pay respect and ask for good favor, a scene we have witnessed over and over again at shrines throughout Japan during our journey.

Hands clap, bells ring—
awaken, dreaming kami!
Dance in Shinto shrines.

After lunch, we walk through the crowded streets of the Okage Yokocho district just outside the shrine area.

Here, local crafts and foods are sold, and musicians and dancers perform in the street. The carnival atmosphere reminds me of the miniature reproductions of Tokugawa streets that were on display in the Edo Tokyo Museum.

As we head toward Naiku, the Inner Shrine, clouds darken the sky, the wind picks up, and rain pours down, giving welcome relief from the heat. However, I remember the strong winds at Shiogama and Matsushima followed by the heavy rain and wind at Haguro-san and Gassan. Are the kami trying to communicate something to us? Luckily, this time the wind dies down, the rain stops almost as quickly as it began, and we are able to continue our climb to the Inner Shrine.

> *On this path, shining*
> *leaves, green stones placed one by one—*
> *steps mindful and slow.*

At the entrance, which is covered by a translucent white curtain, we clap and bow. As I raise my head, the wind blows the curtain just enough to reveal a Shinto priest in ghostly white robes and a black hat giving blessings to one who has paid for the privilege. The curtain closes so quickly I wonder if what I've seen is real. The Inner Shrine shimmers with mystery.

> *Sacred treetops sway—*
> *murmur of ancient voices*
> *in the rising sap.*

It's time to leave the shrine area. I bow and give thanks for my experiences with this land and people, pass my hand over the bark of the giant cedar, and wipe the last drops of rain from a sakaki leaf. May I find in everything I do the same kind of holiness and serenity I have found here.

Back on the street, we walk to Akafuku Sweets and enjoy confections made from the family's 300-year-old recipe. Their tops are a sugared sweet formed like the waves of the Isuzu River which passes by the shop, their bottoms a bean paste that resembles the sand at the river's bottom. A breeze blows in through the open windows above us. Level with the street, the windows afford a view of the hundreds of footsteps passing by.

> *Wind chimes ping—pilgrims*
> *crossing the bridge to Ise—*
> *old festival dreams.*

JULY 26, 2009

Back at Urawa, I am sitting in Starbuck's listening to

Otis Redding's "Sittin' on the Dock of the Bay," reminded, as always, of an old high school friend, now dead for over thirty years, who loved to sing that song. Why does this memory of him stay with me while so many others have not? What memories of this journey will linger with me and which will float away?

I decide to attend a calligraphy exhibit in the Ginza district of Tokyo, where Oishi sensei, who tried so valiantly to teach me calligraphy at the start of our visit, has several pieces. It is a fitting conclusion to this journey that has opened my heart. Would I be better at the art of calligraphy now? I wonder.

Oishi's calligraphy sensei died when he was in his nineties, and now the old sensei's son has become Sensei. People of all ages, from schoolgirls in short skirts and knee socks to conservatively dressed matrons and elderly men leaning on canes, wander through the exhibit rooms. Sensei, who gives generously of his time, explains what makes a piece of calligraphy "great": it must be deep, clear, strong, and balanced. Unlike dance and painting, he suggests, which have a beginning and an end, calligraphy continues to exist in the process revealed in the strokes. Because the strokes have to be done in a certain order, the viewer can retrace the calligrapher's steps, which sometimes are completed in

the space of thirty seconds. Using lessons from the past, one must approach calligraphy with a balance of planned movement and spontaneity born of a strong and open heart. Not bad advice for life, either.

Following footsteps
deep, strong, clear—unity and
balance in process.

I am drawn to a piece that a companion translates as "not one thing." Yes, nothing is ever "one thing."

On our last full day in Japan, I rise early and sit by the garden at the Japan Foundation in Urawa. For the first time, I see blue-tinged fish meandering in the pond. It is purposeful wandering, perhaps. They might want or need food, and yet they move so calmly, so quietly, every motion fluid, their tails and backs rippling the water just a little before it clears and becomes a mirror of the clouds moving in the sky. Minutes later, a ripple is followed by the quiet splash of a leaping fish, which quickly disappears beneath the surface, the water settling to clarity again. Now bubbles form on the surface, yet I can't see the cause. There is so much to see here that I wonder about the need to move on.

> "Just a brief stop,"
> I said when stepping off the road
> into a willow's shade
> where a bubbling stream flows by,
> as has time since my 'brief stop.'"
>
> (Saigyo as translated in LaFleur, 142)

I pack my bags and decide to leave my white Matsushima hat with its dried lavender woven through

the band on a "free for the taking" table at the Foundation. *Jo, ha, kyu, zanshin.* Another journey begins.

On the plane and missing Japan already, I remind myself of Basho's wisdom:

> The moon and the sun are eternal travelers. Even the years wander on. A lifetime adrift in a boat or in old age leading a tired horse into

the years, every day is a journey and the journey itself is home. (as translated by Hamill, 3)

And again of Saigyo:

> Returning to where
> it used to see blossoms,
> my mind, changed,
> will stay at Yoshino,
> home now, and see anew.
>
> (as translated in LaFleur, 119)

And my old companion, T. S. Eliot:

> We shall not cease from exploration
> And the end of all our exploring
> Will be to arrive where we started
> And know the place for the first time.(197)

My heart surrenders to the quiet. Circles within circles. Layer upon layer. I am bringing so much home with me that will change my world. But I've left some things behind, too.

Sweet lavender, whose
fingers touch you now, releasing
Matsushima dreams?

Works Cited

Bok, Gordon, with Ann Mayo Muir and Ed Trickett. *Turning Toward the Morning.* Sharon, CT: Folk-Legacy Records, Inc., 1975.

Eliot, T. S. *The Complete Poems and Plays of T. S. Eliot.* London: Faber and Faber, 1969.

Feiler, Bruce. *Learning to Bow: an American Teacher in a Japanese School.* New York: Ticknor and Fields, 1991.

Hamill, Sam. *Narrow Road to the Interior and Other Writings.* Boston: Shambhala, 1998.

Heyde, Thomas. "Basho and the Aesthetics of Wandering: Recuperating Space, Recognizing Place, and Following the Ways of the Universe" in *Philosophy of East and West,* 53.3 (July 2003). Gale Power Search, 5/27/2008.

Kerr, Alex. *Lost Japan.* Oakland, CA: Lonely Planet, 2009.

LaFleur, William R. *Awesome Nightfall: The Life, Times, and Poetry of Saigyo.* Boston: Wisdom Publications, 2003.

Miner, Earl. *Japanese Poetic Diaries.* Berkeley, CA: University of California Press, 1969.

Oliver, Mary. *House of Light.* Boston, MA: Beacon Press, 1990.

Rodd, Laurel Rasplica, Professor of Japanese, University of Colorado. Unpublished translations.

Sakaki, Nanao. *How To Live on the Planet Earth.* Nobleboro, ME: Blackberry Books, 2013.

Strand, Mark. *Poems: Reasons for Moving, Darker, & the Sargentville Notebook.* New York: Alfred Knopf, 1992.

Ueda, Makoto. *The Master Haiku Poet: Matsuo Basho.* New York: Kodansha International, 1982.